Copyright © 2023 by Michael Jaynes (Author)

This book is protected by copyright law and is intended solely for personal use. Reproduction, distribution, or any other form of use requires the written permission of the author. The information presented in this book is for educational and entertainment purposes only, and while every effort has been made to ensure its accuracy and completeness, no guarantees are made. The author is not providing legal, financial, medical, or professional advice, and readers should consult with a licensed professional before implementing any of the techniques discussed in this book. The content in this book has been sourced from various reliable sources, but readers should exercise their own judgment when using this information. The author is not responsible for any losses, direct or indirect, that may occur from the use of this book, including but not limited to errors, omissions, or inaccuracies.

We hope this book has been informative and helpful on your journey to understanding and celebrating older adults. Thank you for your interest and support!

Title: Winning at Both Ends

Subtitle: The Secrets of Football's Player-Coaches

Series: Champions on and off the Field: The Success Stories of Footballers-Turned-Managers

By Michael Jaynes

"The coach is not the most important person in a football club. The most important person is the player."
Johan Cruyff, Dutch footballer and coach

"A football team is like a piano. You need eight men to carry it and three who can play the damn thing."
Bill Shankly, Liverpool FC manager

"I'm a bloody difficult man to work for because I'm always demanding. That's how you get on in life."
Sir Alex Ferguson, Manchester United

"The best coaches are like magicians. They can see what others can't see and make it happen."
Jose Mourinho, AS Roma FC manager.

"A football coach is not a dictator. He is someone who leads and inspires his players to achieve greatness."
Carlo Ancelotti, Real Madrid CF manager.

"I never expect my players to play a game that I wouldn't play myself."
Diego Simeone, Atletico Madrid FC manager

"The coach's role is to create an environment where players can be the best version of themselves."
Jurgen Klopp, Liverpool FC manager

"I am not a dictator, I am a coach."
Pep Guardiola, Manchester City FC manager

Table of Contents

Introduction 8
- *Why footballers make great coaches* 8
- *The challenges of transitioning from player to coach* 11
- *The benefits of having a player's perspective as a coach* 13

Chapter 1: Johann Cruyff 15
- *Cruyff's playing career and achievements* 15
- *The birth of Total Football* 17
- *The Barcelona Dream Team* 19
- *Coaching philosophy and legacy* 22

Chapter 2: Pep Guardiola 24
- *Guardiola's playing career and achievements* 24
- *The Barcelona dynasty* 26
- *The Bayern Munich years* 29
- *The Manchester City era* 31

Chapter 3: Zinedine Zidane 34
- *Zidane's playing career and achievements* 34
- *The Real Madrid Galacticos* 37
- *The first coaching stint and success in the Champions League* 40
- *The comeback and the three-peat* 42

Chapter 4: Diego Simeone 45

    Simeone's playing career and achievements................... 45

    The transformation of Atletico Madrid 49

    The defensive style and counterattacking prowess 52

    The elusive Champions League trophy 55

Chapter 5: Frank Lampard **58**

    Lampard's playing career and achievements 58

    The transition to coaching at Derby County 60

    The return to Chelsea and the first season in charge 64

    The challenges of managing big-name players 68

Chapter 6: Steven Gerrard **74**

    Gerrard's playing career and achievements 74

    The move to coaching at Rangers 76

    The revival of Rangers and the title win 79

    The future and potential return to Liverpool 82

Chapter 7: Thierry Henry.. **84**

    Henry's playing career and achievements 84

    The journey to coaching and the Monaco debacle 89

    The MLS stint and the Montreal Impact 92

    The return to England and the current role at Aston Villa 95

Conclusion **98**

The common traits and qualities of successful player-coaches 98
The future of player-coaches in football 101
The lessons for aspiring coaches and players alike 104
Key Terms and Definitions 107
Supporting Materials..110

Introduction
Why footballers make great coaches

Football has seen many successful player-coaches over the years. From Johan Cruyff to Pep Guardiola, Zinedine Zidane to Diego Simeone, and Frank Lampard to Steven Gerrard, there are plenty of examples of players who have made the successful transition to coaching. But what is it about footballers that makes them such great coaches?

Footballers have a unique perspective on the game. They have spent their entire careers studying the game, learning from their coaches, and honing their skills on the field. They have seen what works and what doesn't, and they know how to motivate and inspire their teammates. This experience gives them a deep understanding of the game and an ability to see things from a player's perspective, which is crucial when coaching.

Footballers also have a natural leadership ability. As players, they are often the ones who set the tone for their team, both on and off the field. They have to be able to communicate effectively with their teammates, motivate them, and lead by example. These leadership skills translate well to coaching, where they can use their experience and knowledge to guide their team to success.

Another reason why footballers make great coaches is their work ethic. Footballers are some of the most hardworking athletes in the world. They spend countless hours training, studying the game, and working on their skills. This dedication and discipline are essential qualities for a coach to have, as they need to be able to inspire and motivate their players to put in the work required to achieve success.

In addition to their work ethic, footballers also have a deep understanding of the importance of teamwork. As players, they know that success on the field is not just about individual talent but about working together as a team. This understanding is essential for a coach, as they need to be able to build a cohesive team and get their players working together towards a common goal.

Finally, footballers have a passion for the game that is unmatched. They live and breathe football, and this passion is infectious. As coaches, they can use their love for the game to inspire and motivate their players, creating a team that is truly dedicated to achieving success.

In conclusion, footballers make great coaches because of their unique perspective on the game, their natural leadership ability, their work ethic, their understanding of teamwork, and their passion for the game. These qualities make them well-suited to guide and inspire their teams to success on and off the field.

The challenges of transitioning from player to coach

Transitioning from a player to a coach is not an easy task, and footballers who have successfully done it have faced many challenges along the way. One of the biggest challenges is adjusting to a new role, which requires a completely different skill set than playing on the field. Some footballers struggle to make the transition because they are so used to being in the spotlight as players that it is difficult for them to take a step back and focus on developing the team as a whole.

Another challenge is the difficulty of managing former teammates. As a player, you are part of the team and have a specific role to play. As a coach, you are responsible for managing the entire team and ensuring that everyone is working together towards a common goal. This can be especially challenging when you are coaching players who used to be your teammates, as there may be tension or resentment if they feel like you are overstepping your bounds.

Coaches who were former players also face challenges when it comes to developing their own coaching style. While they may have learned a lot from their own coaches during their playing career, they must also find their own voice and coaching philosophy. This can be a difficult process, and it takes time to develop a coaching style that works for you and your team.

In addition, there are practical challenges that come with transitioning from player to coach, such as the need to obtain coaching certifications and licenses. This can be time-consuming and expensive, and it can take years to complete all of the necessary training.

Despite these challenges, many footballers have successfully made the transition from player to coach and have gone on to achieve great success. By drawing on their experience as players and developing their coaching skills, they have been able to lead their teams to victory and make a lasting impact on the sport.

The benefits of having a player's perspective as a coach

When a former football player transitions to a coaching role, they bring with them a unique perspective and set of experiences that can be invaluable in the coaching world. In this section, we'll explore some of the benefits of having a player's perspective as a coach.

Firstly, players turn coaches understand what it takes to be successful on the field. They have lived and breathed football for years and have a deep understanding of the game's nuances. As coaches, they can use this knowledge to their advantage, helping their players to develop their skills and strategies to win games.

Secondly, former players can relate to their players in a way that non-players may not be able to. They understand the pressures and challenges that come with being a professional footballer and can empathize with their players' struggles. This allows them to build better relationships with their players, which can lead to more effective communication and teamwork on the field.

Thirdly, players who become coaches often have a deep love and passion for the game. They understand the importance of hard work, dedication, and perseverance, and they can instill these values in their players. This can help to create a winning mentality and a culture of excellence within a team.

Finally, former players can bring a fresh perspective to coaching. They have experienced the game from a player's point of view, and this can help them to see the game in a different way. They may be able to identify weaknesses in their opponents' game or come up with innovative new strategies to help their team win.

In conclusion, having a player's perspective as a coach can be incredibly beneficial for both the coach and their team. Former players have a deep understanding of the game, can relate to their players on a personal level, bring a passion for the game, and can offer a fresh perspective. This is why many former players have gone on to become successful coaches, and why they will continue to be an important part of the footballing world for years to come.

Chapter 1: Johann Cruyff

Cruyff's playing career and achievements

Johan Cruyff is one of the most iconic footballers of all time. His playing career spanned two decades, during which he achieved numerous accolades and left an indelible mark on the sport. This chapter will explore the highlights of Cruyff's playing career and the impact he had on the game.

Cruyff was born in Amsterdam in 1947 and grew up playing street football. He quickly caught the attention of scouts and was signed by Ajax Amsterdam at the age of 10. He made his first-team debut for Ajax at the age of 17, in 1964, and quickly established himself as a key player.

During his time at Ajax, Cruyff won numerous domestic and European titles. He was a three-time winner of the Ballon d'Or, awarded to the best player in Europe, and was instrumental in the Dutch national team's run to the World Cup final in 1974. His playing style was characterized by exceptional technique, vision, and creativity, and he was a master of the "Total Football" system that Ajax and the Netherlands became famous for.

After leaving Ajax, Cruyff played for a brief stint at Barcelona before moving to the United States to play for the Los Angeles Aztecs. He returned to Europe in 1981 to play for Levante in Spain before ending his career at Ajax in 1984.

Cruyff's achievements on the field were remarkable, but his impact on the game went far beyond his playing career. He was a pioneer of the concept of "football as a language," emphasizing the importance of communication and understanding between players. He was also a proponent of attacking football and encouraged his teams to play with flair and creativity.

Cruyff's influence on the game continued into his coaching career, which will be explored in later chapters. But his legacy as a player is secure, and his impact on football is still felt today.

The birth of Total Football

Total Football is a style of play that was born in the Netherlands in the 1970s and is closely associated with Johan Cruyff. The concept behind Total Football is that all players on the field can play in any position, and the emphasis is on fluid movement, quick passing, and constant positional interchange.

Cruyff was instrumental in developing and popularizing Total Football. His experience playing in various positions on the field, including as a striker, attacking midfielder, and winger, allowed him to see the game from a different perspective than many other players and coaches. He saw the potential for a more fluid, dynamic style of play that was less focused on rigid positions and more focused on constant movement and interchange.

Cruyff's vision for Total Football was realized on the field during his time with Ajax Amsterdam, where he won numerous league titles, domestic cups, and European trophies, including three consecutive European Cups from 1971 to 1973. Ajax's success under Cruyff's leadership was built on the principles of Total Football, which allowed the team to dominate opponents with their fluid, dynamic style of play.

Total Football also had a profound impact on the game beyond the Netherlands, influencing coaches and players around the world. Many of the most successful teams in modern football, including Barcelona and Spain's national team, have employed variations of Total Football in their play.

The birth of Total Football was a significant moment in football history, and it was largely thanks to the vision and leadership of Johan Cruyff. His innovative ideas and willingness to experiment with new approaches to the game helped revolutionize football and set the stage for the modern game we know today.

The Barcelona Dream Team

Johan Cruyff's tenure as a player and manager at Barcelona is one of the most iconic and successful periods in the club's history. Under his leadership, the team achieved an unprecedented level of success and redefined the way football was played.

Cruyff joined Barcelona as a player in 1973 and immediately had a major impact on the team. He led the club to their first La Liga title in 14 years in his debut season, and then again in 1974. But it was his influence off the pitch that truly transformed the club.

Cruyff introduced a new playing philosophy that emphasized possession, fluidity, and attacking play. This was the birth of Total Football, a style of play that had been developed by the Dutch national team in the 1970s and was based on the idea that every player on the team should be comfortable playing in any position.

Cruyff's philosophy was implemented at Barcelona through a series of youth academy reforms and signings of key players who fit his style of play, such as Ronald Koeman and Hristo Stoichkov. The result was a team that dominated Spanish football, winning four consecutive La Liga titles between 1991 and 1994.

But the pinnacle of Cruyff's success at Barcelona came in 1992 when the team won the European Cup for the first time in the club's history. The final, played at Wembley Stadium in London, saw Barcelona defeat Sampdoria 1-0 thanks to a stunning free-kick from Ronald Koeman. The team was composed of legendary players such as Romário, Hristo Stoichkov, and Pep Guardiola, and their performance in the final is still remembered as one of the greatest displays of attacking football in the history of the game.

Cruyff's influence at Barcelona continued long after his playing and managerial career at the club ended. His playing philosophy, based on possession and attacking play, became synonymous with the club and has been passed down through generations of Barcelona players and coaches. The current coach, Ronald Koeman, was one of Cruyff's key signings in 1989 and has openly acknowledged the influence that Cruyff had on his own coaching career.

In conclusion, Johan Cruyff's impact on Barcelona cannot be overstated. His playing career, managerial success, and pioneering approach to the game have left an indelible mark on one of the world's greatest football clubs. The Barcelona Dream Team of the early 1990s will always be remembered as one of the greatest teams in football history, and Johan Cruyff will forever be remembered as the architect of their success.

Coaching philosophy and legacy

Johann Cruyff's impact on football extended beyond his playing career and the success of his Barcelona Dream Team. His innovative approach to coaching and his philosophy on the game have influenced generations of players and coaches alike.

Cruyff believed in a style of play that emphasized possession, fluid movement, and creative expression. He called it "Total Football," and it was a departure from the more rigid and structured approach to the game that was popular at the time. Total Football required players to be versatile, able to switch positions seamlessly, and comfortable on the ball. It was a style of play that demanded both technical and tactical excellence, and it required a deep understanding of the game.

Cruyff's coaching philosophy was built on the principles of Total Football. He believed that the game should be played with joy and creativity, that players should be given the freedom to express themselves, and that success could be achieved by playing beautiful, attacking football. He also placed great importance on developing young players and creating a cohesive team spirit. He believed that the team was more important than any individual player, and that success could only be achieved through hard work and discipline.

Cruyff's legacy as a coach is significant. He went on to coach Barcelona, where he won four La Liga titles and the club's first-ever European Cup. He also coached the Netherlands national team, taking them to the 1994 World Cup quarter-finals. He inspired a generation of Dutch coaches, including Louis van Gaal, Frank Rijkaard, and Ronald Koeman, who have all gone on to achieve success at the highest level of the game.

Cruyff's impact on the game of football cannot be overstated. His Total Football philosophy and innovative coaching approach have changed the way the game is played and coached. His legacy continues to inspire coaches and players around the world, and his influence can be seen in the way the game is played today.

Chapter 2: Pep Guardiola

Guardiola's playing career and achievements

Pep Guardiola's playing career was marked by tremendous success, and his achievements as a player laid the foundation for his later success as a coach.

Guardiola was born in Santpedor, Catalonia, in 1971. He began playing football at a young age and quickly showed promise as a talented midfielder. At the age of 13, he joined FC Barcelona's youth academy, La Masia, where he began to develop his skills as a player.

Guardiola made his first-team debut for Barcelona in 1990, at the age of 19. Over the next decade, he established himself as one of the best midfielders in the world, winning numerous trophies and accolades along the way.

One of Guardiola's most significant achievements as a player was helping Barcelona win the UEFA Champions League in 1992. Guardiola was an instrumental part of the team that defeated Sampdoria in the final, playing a key role in Barcelona's midfield.

Guardiola also had success with the Spanish national team, helping Spain win the gold medal at the 1992 Summer Olympics in Barcelona. He later played for Spain at the 1994 World Cup in the United States, where he helped the team reach the quarterfinals.

Guardiola spent most of his playing career with Barcelona, but he also had stints with other clubs. He played for Italian clubs Brescia and Roma before finishing his playing career with Al-Ahli in Qatar.

Overall, Guardiola's playing career was marked by his incredible vision, creativity, and technical ability. He was known for his passing range, his ability to control the tempo of the game, and his intelligence on the field.

Guardiola's success as a player provided the foundation for his later success as a coach. His playing career gave him a deep understanding of the game, and he was able to use that understanding to develop innovative coaching strategies and tactics.

Guardiola's ability to combine his playing experience with his coaching knowledge has made him one of the most successful coaches in the history of the sport. His understanding of the game and his ability to develop and implement new ideas has helped him win numerous titles and establish a legacy as one of the game's greats.

The Barcelona dynasty

The Barcelona dynasty is one of the most successful and celebrated eras in football history. Led by Pep Guardiola as a coach, the team was renowned for its dominance on the pitch, playing an attractive, possession-based style of football that came to be known as "tiki-taka." But the dynasty was built on more than just tactics; it was rooted in a strong team culture and a shared philosophy that emphasized hard work, humility, and unity.

Guardiola took over as coach of Barcelona in 2008, inheriting a team that had finished third in La Liga the previous season. He immediately set about implementing his vision for the team, which was centered around a possession-based style of play that emphasized short, quick passes and movement off the ball. The team's first season under Guardiola was a resounding success, as they won the treble (La Liga, Copa del Rey, and UEFA Champions League) and established themselves as one of the best teams in the world.

The Barcelona dynasty was characterized by its dominant performances on the pitch, as the team won an unprecedented 14 trophies in just four seasons under Guardiola's leadership. But it was also defined by its strong team culture, which emphasized values such as hard work, humility, and unity. Guardiola was known for his attention to detail and his demanding coaching style, which helped to create a team that was highly disciplined and committed to its collective goals.

The team's success was also due in large part to the individual talents of its players, many of whom were products of the club's renowned youth academy, La Masia. Players such as Lionel Messi, Xavi, and Andres Iniesta became synonymous with the Barcelona dynasty, helping to establish the team's reputation as one of the greatest in football history.

Guardiola's tenure at Barcelona came to an end in 2012, but the legacy of the dynasty lives on. The team's style of play, which emphasized possession and teamwork, has become an inspiration for coaches around the world. And Guardiola himself has gone on to enjoy success at other clubs, including Bayern Munich and Manchester City, where he has continued to implement his vision for the game.

In conclusion, the Barcelona dynasty under Guardiola was a remarkable period of success for both the team and the coach. Guardiola's playing career may have been overshadowed by the likes of Johan Cruyff and Lionel Messi, but his achievements as a coach are second to none. The dynasty was built on a strong team culture and a shared philosophy that emphasized hard work, humility, and unity, and it will be remembered as one of the greatest eras in football history.

The Bayern Munich years

Pep Guardiola's tenure as Bayern Munich's head coach was marked by continued success and dominance in the Bundesliga. Guardiola took over the reins at Bayern Munich in 2013 after a sabbatical year following his departure from Barcelona. He inherited a team that had just won the treble, and the pressure was on him to maintain the high standards set by his predecessor, Jupp Heynckes.

In his first season at Bayern, Guardiola implemented his trademark possession-based style of play, which had brought him so much success at Barcelona. He made several tactical adjustments to the team's formation, moving Philipp Lahm from right-back to midfield, and David Alaba from left-back to center-back. These changes allowed Bayern to control possession and dominate opponents, while also providing more attacking options from deep midfield areas.

Guardiola's Bayern side won the Bundesliga title in his first season with a record 90 points and finished 19 points ahead of their nearest rivals. They also reached the semi-finals of the Champions League, where they were knocked out by eventual champions Real Madrid. Guardiola's second season was similarly successful, as Bayern retained their Bundesliga title and reached the semi-finals of the Champions League once again. However, they were eliminated by Barcelona, Guardiola's former club.

Guardiola's third and final season at Bayern was arguably his most challenging, as the team struggled with injuries and fatigue. Despite this, Bayern managed to win the Bundesliga title for the third consecutive season. However, they were once again eliminated from the Champions League at the semi-final stage, this time by Atletico Madrid. Guardiola left Bayern Munich at the end of the season, having won three Bundesliga titles, two DFB-Pokal cups, and reached three semi-finals in the Champions League.

Guardiola's time at Bayern Munich was characterized by his ability to maintain the team's dominance in the Bundesliga while also implementing his own style of play. He was able to adapt his tactics to suit the players at his disposal, while also introducing new ideas and concepts to the team. Guardiola's Bayern Munich was a well-oiled machine, capable of dominating possession and scoring goals with ease. His success at Bayern cemented his status as one of the best coaches in the world and paved the way for his move to Manchester City.

The Manchester City era

Pep Guardiola's move to Manchester City in 2016 was highly anticipated by football fans and pundits alike. After a year-long sabbatical, the Spanish coach returned to the game and took on one of the biggest challenges of his career: rebuilding a team that had underperformed in recent seasons.

Guardiola's arrival at City marked a new era for the club, which had never won the Champions League and had only won two Premier League titles in the past decade. His reputation as one of the best coaches in the world preceded him, and expectations were high.

The first season was a learning curve for both Guardiola and his players. The Catalan coach implemented his trademark possession-based style of play, but it took time for the squad to adjust to his demands. City finished third in the league, 15 points behind champions Chelsea, and were knocked out of the Champions League in the round of 16 by Monaco.

Guardiola wasted no time in the summer transfer window, bringing in new signings such as Bernardo Silva, Kyle Walker, and Ederson. The following season, City dominated the Premier League, setting a new points record of 100 and winning the title with five games to spare.

Guardiola's side played with a fluidity and attacking verve that had not been seen in English football for years.

City also reached the quarter-finals of the Champions League that season, but were knocked out by Liverpool. Guardiola was criticized for overthinking the tactics in that game, but his response was typical of his approach to coaching: "I will do it again."

The 2018-19 season saw Guardiola face new challenges, as Liverpool emerged as City's main title rivals. The title race went down to the wire, with City pipping the Merseyside club to the trophy by a single point. City also won the FA Cup, completing an unprecedented domestic treble.

However, the Champions League continued to elude Guardiola at City. Despite reaching the quarter-finals once again, his side were knocked out by Tottenham in dramatic fashion. Guardiola was left to rue missed chances and defensive lapses, but remained determined to learn from the experience and improve.

The 2019-20 season was disrupted by the Covid-19 pandemic, but Guardiola still managed to guide City to a second-place finish in the Premier League and the semi-finals of the Champions League. The following season, City were unstoppable, winning the league by a margin of 12 points and reaching the Champions League final for the first time in the club's history.

Although City were beaten 1-0 by Chelsea in the final, Guardiola's influence on the team was clear. His tactical adjustments, such as playing without a recognized striker, had helped City to dominate their opponents throughout the tournament.

Guardiola's time at City has been characterized by his commitment to playing attacking football and his willingness to experiment with new formations and tactics. He has also shown a willingness to adapt to the demands of the English game, incorporating a more direct style of play when necessary.

His success at City has cemented his place as one of the greatest coaches of his generation, and his legacy at the club will be remembered for years to come.

Chapter 3: Zinedine Zidane

Zidane's playing career and achievements

Zinedine Zidane is widely regarded as one of the greatest footballers of all time, known for his technical ability, vision, and composure on the ball. He had an illustrious playing career that spanned over a decade, during which he won numerous individual awards and helped his teams achieve great success.

Early Career

Born on June 23, 1972, in Marseille, France, Zidane was the youngest of five children in a family of Algerian descent. He started playing football at a young age and quickly demonstrated his talent. He joined the youth academy at AS Cannes and made his professional debut for the club in 1989 at the age of 17. In 1992, he was signed by Bordeaux, where he spent four seasons and established himself as one of the top midfielders in France.

World Cup Triumph and Move to Juventus

Zidane's breakthrough on the international stage came during the 1998 FIFA World Cup, which was hosted by France. He played a crucial role in the French team's success, scoring two goals in the final against Brazil to help his country win their first World Cup. His performances during the tournament earned him the Golden Ball award for the best player.

Following the World Cup, Zidane attracted interest from some of the biggest clubs in Europe, and in 1996 he signed with Juventus. He spent five seasons with the Italian giants, during which he won two Serie A titles and reached the UEFA Champions League final twice, winning the trophy in 1996.

Galacticos Era at Real Madrid

In 2001, Zidane was signed by Real Madrid for a then-world record transfer fee of €77.5 million. He joined a team that already had some of the biggest names in world football, including Luis Figo, Ronaldo, and Roberto Carlos. Zidane quickly became a key player for Real Madrid and helped them win their ninth UEFA Champions League title in his first season at the club.

Zidane continued to play a pivotal role in the Real Madrid team that became known as the Galacticos. He won La Liga in 2003 and reached the Champions League final again in 2004, although they lost to Porto in a shock upset. Zidane retired from international football after the 2004 European Championships, but continued to play for Real Madrid until 2006.

Retirement and Legacy

Zidane retired from football after the 2006 FIFA World Cup, which was held in Germany. His final game for the French national team was the final of the tournament, where he was sent off for head-butting Italian defender Marco Materazzi. Despite the controversial ending to his playing career, Zidane's legacy as one of the greatest footballers of all time was already secured.

Zidane won numerous individual awards during his playing career, including the Ballon d'Or in 1998, 2000, and 2003. He was also named FIFA World Player of the Year in 1998, 2000, and 2003. Zidane's elegant style of play, combined with his ability to score important goals in big games, made him a fan favorite and an icon of the sport.

As a coach, Zidane has continued to build on his legacy. After a successful stint as Real Madrid Castilla manager, he was appointed as the first-team coach in January 2016. In his first season in charge, he led Real Madrid to the UEFA Champions League title, becoming the first coach to win the trophy in his debut season. He went on to win the Champions League three times in a row, as well as a La Liga title and two FIFA Club World Cup trophies, before leaving the club in 2018.

The Real Madrid Galacticos

Zinedine Zidane's playing career was nothing short of spectacular, but his success as a coach has been equally impressive. One of the most notable periods of his coaching career was during his time at Real Madrid, where he led the club to three consecutive Champions League titles. This period coincided with the arrival of the "Galacticos," a group of star players who were signed for exorbitant sums of money.

The Galacticos era began in 2000 when Florentino Perez became Real Madrid's president. Perez was a businessman who had made his fortune in the construction industry, and he was determined to turn Real Madrid into the most glamorous and successful club in the world. He set his sights on signing the biggest stars in world football, and he was willing to pay whatever it took to get them.

The first major signing of the Galacticos era was Zidane himself. Real Madrid paid a then-world record fee of €75 million to sign the French midfielder from Juventus. Zidane had already won the World Cup and the Ballon d'Or, and he was widely regarded as one of the best players in the world.

Zidane was followed by a string of other high-profile signings, including Ronaldo, David Beckham, and Luis Figo.

These players were signed for eye-watering sums of money, and they quickly became the most famous and glamorous team in the world.

The Galacticos era was not without its successes. Real Madrid won the Champions League in 2002, and they won La Liga in 2003. Zidane was a key player in both of these triumphs, and he formed a formidable midfield partnership with the Brazilian superstar Ronaldo.

However, the Galacticos era was also marked by a lack of success. Real Madrid went three years without winning a major trophy between 2004 and 2007, despite the presence of some of the best players in the world. The team was criticized for lacking cohesion and team spirit, and there were rumors of rifts between the players.

When Zidane took over as Real Madrid's coach in 2016, he inherited a team that was once again filled with star players. However, he was determined to learn from the mistakes of the Galacticos era and build a team that was greater than the sum of its parts.

Under Zidane's leadership, Real Madrid won three consecutive Champions League titles between 2016 and 2018. The team played with a level of intensity and cohesion that had been lacking during the Galacticos era, and Zidane was praised for his tactical acumen and man-management skills.

Zidane's success as a coach has been built on the lessons he learned during his playing career. He was a player who valued hard work and teamwork above individual brilliance, and he has brought those values to his coaching career. He has also been able to use his experience as a Galactico to understand the pressures and expectations that come with coaching a team of star players.

The Real Madrid Galacticos may have been a symbol of excess and glamour, but Zidane's success as a coach has shown that even the most talented and expensive players need a strong team ethic and a clear tactical plan to achieve success.

The first coaching stint and success in the Champions League

After retiring from football, Zinedine Zidane began his coaching career with Real Madrid's youth teams. In 2016, he was appointed as the first-team coach, replacing Rafael Benitez. Zidane took over a team that was struggling in La Liga, but he immediately made an impact by leading them to their 11th Champions League title in his first season in charge.

Zidane's success in the Champions League was not just down to luck. He implemented a number of changes to the team's style of play that helped them become more effective in the competition. One of the most significant changes was his decision to switch from a 4-3-3 formation to a 4-4-2 diamond formation. This change allowed Real Madrid to control the midfield and give their attacking players more freedom to create chances.

Zidane's man-management skills were also crucial to his success in the Champions League. He had a great relationship with his players and was able to get the best out of them. He also made some bold decisions, such as starting Isco in the final against Juventus, which paid off handsomely.

Real Madrid's success in the Champions League did not stop there. Zidane went on to win the competition in the next two seasons as well, becoming the first coach to win the Champions League three times in a row since the tournament was rebranded in 1992. This incredible achievement solidified Zidane's place as one of the greatest coaches in the history of the competition.

In addition to his success in the Champions League, Zidane also led Real Madrid to a La Liga title in the 2016-17 season. This was the first time Real Madrid had won the league since 2012, and it was a testament to Zidane's ability to motivate his players and get them to perform at their best.

Zidane's first coaching stint at Real Madrid was a huge success, and it cemented his reputation as one of the best young coaches in the game. His ability to make tactical adjustments, his man-management skills, and his ability to get the best out of his players were all key factors in his success. But it was also clear that Zidane had a deep understanding of Real Madrid's culture and history, and he was able to use this to his advantage in his coaching.

The comeback and the three-peat

Zinedine Zidane's first stint as Real Madrid manager was a resounding success, but it was his comeback to the club in 2019 that would go down in history. After a tumultuous 2018-19 season that saw Real Madrid finish third in La Liga and exit the Champions League in the Round of 16, Zidane was brought back to the club in March 2019 to restore order and bring back success.

Zidane's return was met with skepticism by many, who questioned whether he could recreate the magic of his first tenure at the club. However, he quickly set to work, making some key signings and implementing his trademark style of play. Real Madrid finished the season on a high, winning their last 11 games in a row to secure a third-place finish in the league and a spot in the Champions League for the following season.

The 2019-20 season started off in promising fashion, with Real Madrid sitting at the top of the league table for much of the campaign. However, the COVID-19 pandemic put a halt to the season for several months, and when play resumed, it was clear that the break had affected some teams more than others. Real Madrid, however, were able to maintain their momentum and eventually secured their 34th

La Liga title, finishing five points ahead of second-place Barcelona.

But it was in the Champions League that Zidane and his team truly shone. Real Madrid had won the competition in each of the previous three seasons under Zidane's leadership, and they were determined to make it four in a row. They started the campaign off slowly, with a 3-0 loss to Paris Saint-Germain in the opening group stage game, but they quickly regrouped and won their remaining five group stage matches to finish top of their group.

In the knockout stages, Real Madrid faced tough opponents in the form of Manchester City, Atalanta, and Chelsea. But Zidane's tactical acumen and his team's resilience saw them overcome each challenge. They beat Manchester City 4-2 on aggregate in the Round of 16, Atalanta 4-1 on aggregate in the quarterfinals, and Chelsea 3-1 in the semifinals to book their spot in the final.

The final, which was played in Lisbon, pitted Real Madrid against French champions Paris Saint-Germain. Many pundits predicted a close and hard-fought contest, but Real Madrid dominated from start to finish, winning 3-0 thanks to goals from Karim Benzema and Gareth Bale. The victory was Zidane's fourth Champions League title as a manager, and Real Madrid's 13th overall.

Zidane's success in the Champions League is a testament to his ability to manage big games and get the best out of his players when it matters most. His calm demeanor and tactical flexibility are key attributes that have helped him succeed at the highest level of European football. And with his team looking stronger than ever, it wouldn't be surprising to see Zidane and Real Madrid lift the Champions League trophy once again in the near future.

Chapter 4: Diego Simeone

Simeone's playing career and achievements

Diego Simeone, commonly known as "El Cholo," is a retired Argentine footballer and current coach of Atletico Madrid. Simeone is regarded as one of the best defensive midfielders of his generation and has had a successful career both as a player and a coach.

Simeone was born on April 28, 1970, in Buenos Aires, Argentina. He began his football career at the age of nine at the Velez Sarsfield academy. Simeone made his professional debut for Velez Sarsfield in 1987 at the age of 17. He played for Velez Sarsfield for four years, winning the Argentine Primera Division twice in 1993 and 1996.

In 1992, Simeone made his international debut for Argentina and played a crucial role in helping Argentina win the Copa America in 1992 and 1993. He also played in the 1994 World Cup, where Argentina reached the Round of 16.

Simeone's playing style was characterized by his tenacity, energy, and ability to read the game. He was known for his hard tackling, excellent passing range, and tactical awareness. Simeone was also an excellent leader on and off the pitch, and he often inspired his teammates with his never-say-die attitude.

After playing for Velez Sarsfield, Simeone went on to play for Italian giants Inter Milan, where he won the UEFA Cup in 1998. He then moved to Lazio in 1999, where he won the Serie A title and the Coppa Italia in the 1999-2000 season.

In 2003, Simeone returned to Argentina to play for River Plate, where he won the Argentine Primera Division in 2004. He retired from football in 2006 after a brief stint with Racing Club.

Simeone's playing career was a successful one, with numerous domestic and international titles to his name. He played for some of the biggest clubs in the world, and his tenacity, leadership, and tactical awareness on the pitch made him a fan favorite.

After retiring from football, Simeone began his coaching career. He started his coaching journey at Racing Club in 2006, where he won the Argentine Primera Division in the 2006 Apertura. He then coached Estudiantes de La Plata, where he won the Argentine Primera Division in the 2006 Apertura and the Copa Libertadores in 2009.

Simeone's biggest success as a coach came when he joined Atletico Madrid in 2011. In his first full season in charge, he led Atletico Madrid to the UEFA Europa League title and the UEFA Super Cup in 2012. In the 2013-14 season, Simeone led Atletico Madrid to their first La Liga title in 18 years and also guided them to the Champions League final, where they were beaten by city rivals Real Madrid.

Despite that defeat, Simeone's impact on Atletico Madrid was immense. He transformed the team into a well-drilled defensive unit and made them one of the toughest teams to beat in Europe. His tactics were built around a solid defense and quick counter-attacking play, and he instilled a winning mentality in his players.

Simeone's achievements as a coach have not gone unnoticed, and he has won several awards for his coaching. In 2013, he was named the La Liga Coach of the Year, and in 2014, he was named the Globe Soccer Awards Coach of the Year.

Continuation:

Simeone's impressive achievements as a coach have not only earned him awards, but also admiration from fellow coaches, players, and fans. His tactical approach and intense coaching style have been lauded by many as instrumental in Atletico Madrid's success.

One of the standout features of Simeone's coaching style is his emphasis on defensive organization and discipline. He has been known to deploy a high-pressing system that makes it difficult for opponents to break through his team's defense. Simeone's Atletico Madrid teams are renowned for their defensive solidity, and this has been a major factor in their success over the years.

Another hallmark of Simeone's coaching is his ability to get the best out of his players. He is known for his man-management skills and his ability to motivate his players to give their all on the field. Simeone is not afraid to make bold decisions, such as dropping star players or playing with a more defensive setup, if he feels it will benefit the team.

Simeone's success at Atletico Madrid has not gone unnoticed, and he has been linked with several high-profile coaching jobs over the years. However, he has remained loyal to Atletico Madrid and has continued to build on the success he has achieved with the club.

Overall, Diego Simeone's achievements as a coach are a testament to his tactical acumen, man-management skills, and unwavering commitment to his team's success. He has shown that a successful coach does not need to have a glittering playing career, but rather a deep understanding of the game, a clear vision for the team, and the ability to get the best out of his players.

The transformation of Atletico Madrid

Diego Simeone's greatest achievement as a coach has been his transformation of Atletico Madrid. When he took over as the manager in 2011, Atletico was a team that had been struggling in mid-table for several seasons. However, in just a few short years, Simeone turned them into one of the most successful and feared teams in Europe.

One of the key reasons for Simeone's success at Atletico has been his ability to instill a winning mentality in his players. From the very beginning, Simeone made it clear that he expected nothing but the best from his team, and he demanded a level of effort and intensity from them that few other coaches could match. He created a culture of hard work and discipline at the club, and his players responded by giving their all on the pitch.

Simeone's tactical acumen has also been a major factor in Atletico's success. He has developed a highly effective defensive system that has become known as the "Cholismo" style of play. This system is built around a compact defensive structure that is incredibly difficult to break down, and it relies heavily on quick counter-attacks to score goals. Simeone's teams are well-drilled and highly organized, and they have proven to be extremely difficult to beat.

Another key factor in Simeone's success at Atletico has been his ability to identify and develop talent. He has a keen eye for young players who have the potential to become stars, and he has been very successful at nurturing that talent and helping it to flourish. Players like Antoine Griezmann, Diego Costa, and Jan Oblak have all thrived under Simeone's tutelage, and he has helped to turn them into some of the best players in the world.

One of the defining moments of Simeone's time at Atletico came in the 2013-14 season, when he led the club to the La Liga title. This was the first time Atletico had won the league since 1996, and it was a huge achievement for the club. Simeone's team played some of the best football in Europe that season, and they were incredibly difficult to beat. The title was secured on the final day of the season, when they held Barcelona to a 1-1 draw at the Camp Nou, sparking wild celebrations from the Atletico fans.

However, Simeone's greatest achievement at Atletico came in the 2013-14 UEFA Champions League. Atletico had been drawn in a tough group, alongside Zenit St Petersburg, Porto, and Austria Wien. However, they emerged as group winners, and they went on to beat AC Milan, Barcelona, and Chelsea on their way to the final in Lisbon. There, they faced their city rivals Real Madrid, who were the overwhelming favorites to win the game. However, Simeone's team put in a magnificent performance, and they were just a few minutes away from securing a famous victory. Unfortunately for Atletico, Real Madrid scored a last-minute equalizer, and they went on to win the game 4-1 in extra time. It was a heartbreaking defeat for Atletico, but it was a testament to Simeone's coaching ability that he had taken a team that was not expected to compete at the highest level and turned them into genuine contenders.

      Since that defeat in the Champions League final, Simeone has continued to build on his success at Atletico. He has won the Europa League twice, and he has guided the club to several more top-four finishes in La Liga. He has also overseen a major overhaul of the squad, bringing in a new generation of players who have continued to excel under his guidance.

The defensive style and counterattacking prowess

Diego Simeone's Atletico Madrid is known for their defensive style of play and counterattacking prowess. The team is often referred to as a "Cholismo" team, named after Simeone's nickname "Cholo." The style of play is characterized by a deep-lying block of players, intense pressing, and quick transitions from defense to attack.

One of the key components of Atletico's defensive strategy is their organization without the ball. The team is well-drilled in maintaining a compact shape that is difficult for opponents to penetrate. Simeone's team is often seen defending in a 4-4-2 formation, with two banks of four defenders and midfielders, and two forwards who are responsible for pressing the opposition's defenders. The players are disciplined and work together as a unit to cut off passing lanes and prevent the opposition from advancing into dangerous areas.

Atletico Madrid's defensive approach has been extremely effective, as they have consistently been one of the best defensive teams in Europe. In the 2013-2014 season, they conceded only 26 goals in 38 La Liga matches, and in the 2015-2016 season, they conceded just 18 goals in 38 La Liga matches. Their defensive solidity has been instrumental in their success under Simeone.

Another important aspect of Atletico's style of play is their ability to transition quickly from defense to attack. Once they win the ball back, they look to break quickly and catch their opponents off guard. The team is quick and direct in their play, with forwards like Antoine Griezmann and Diego Costa leading the charge. Simeone's team is also dangerous on set-pieces, where they often look to capitalize on their height advantage and physicality.

Atletico Madrid's style of play has been successful under Simeone, as evidenced by their numerous titles and accomplishments. In the 2013-2014 season, they won the La Liga title, breaking the dominance of Real Madrid and Barcelona. They also reached the final of the UEFA Champions League that season, only to be beaten by their city rivals Real Madrid. However, they would get their revenge two years later, as they beat Real Madrid in the final of the 2015-2016 Champions League. Atletico has also won the Europa League three times under Simeone, in 2012, 2018, and 2022.

Simeone's defensive style of play has drawn criticism from some quarters, with detractors accusing him of being overly defensive and negative. However, Simeone has defended his approach, stating that he is simply doing what is necessary to win. His players have also spoken highly of his coaching methods, praising his intensity and attention to detail.

In conclusion, Diego Simeone's Atletico Madrid is known for their defensive style of play and counterattacking prowess. Simeone's team is well-drilled in maintaining a compact shape without the ball, and they are quick to transition from defense to attack. This approach has been successful, as Atletico Madrid has won numerous titles under Simeone, including the La Liga, Europa League, and UEFA Champions League. While some critics may view Simeone's approach as overly defensive, his players have spoken highly of his coaching methods, and his success speaks for itself.

The elusive Champions League trophy

Diego Simeone has had great success with Atletico Madrid, leading them to multiple domestic titles and even a Europa League trophy. However, the one trophy that has eluded him and the club is the Champions League.

The Champions League has always been a coveted trophy for Atletico Madrid, and Simeone's tenure at the club has brought them closer than ever before. In fact, Simeone has led Atletico Madrid to two Champions League finals, in 2014 and 2016, but unfortunately, they lost both.

The 2014 final was played against their city rivals, Real Madrid, and it was a tightly contested match that ended in a 1-1 draw after extra time. The match went to penalties, and Atletico Madrid seemed to be on the brink of their first Champions League victory when they took a 1-0 lead. However, Real Madrid came back to win the shootout 4-1, leaving Simeone and his players devastated.

The 2016 final was played against Real Madrid again, and this time it was a repeat of the 2014 final. Once again, the match was tightly contested, and it ended in a 1-1 draw after extra time. However, this time, Real Madrid was able to win the shootout 5-3, leaving Atletico Madrid and Simeone heartbroken once again.

Despite the two disappointments, Simeone has not given up on his dream of winning the Champions League with Atletico Madrid. He has continued to build a strong team, and they have consistently qualified for the competition every year.

In the 2019-20 season, Atletico Madrid was once again in the competition, and they had a strong showing in the group stage. They finished second in their group, behind Juventus, and advanced to the knockout stage.

In the Round of 16, they faced Liverpool, the reigning Champions League winners, and one of the favorites to win the competition. Atletico Madrid was able to pull off a stunning upset, winning the tie 4-2 on aggregate.

In the quarterfinals, they faced RB Leipzig, and once again, they were able to come out on top, winning the tie 2-1. This set up a semifinal matchup against Paris Saint-Germain, another strong team that was considered one of the favorites to win the competition.

The semifinal was a tightly contested match, but unfortunately for Atletico Madrid and Simeone, PSG was able to win 3-0, ending their Champions League run for the season.

Despite the disappointment, Simeone and his team continue to chase their dream of winning the Champions

League. The elusive trophy is still within their reach, and Simeone's tactical acumen and his ability to motivate his players will be crucial if they are to finally lift the trophy.

Chapter 5: Frank Lampard

Lampard's playing career and achievements

Frank Lampard is a former English professional footballer who enjoyed a glittering career both domestically and internationally. Lampard began his career at West Ham United, where he spent seven years before moving on to Chelsea in 2001.

During his playing career, Lampard won numerous individual and team accolades. He was a three-time Premier League winner with Chelsea and also helped the club win four FA Cups, two League Cups, and the UEFA Europa League. In addition to his domestic success, Lampard also enjoyed a successful international career with England, earning 106 caps and scoring 29 goals.

Lampard was known for his outstanding technical ability, intelligence on the pitch, and his incredible work ethic. He was also a prolific scorer for a midfielder, finishing his career with over 300 goals in all competitions. Lampard's incredible performances on the pitch earned him numerous individual awards, including the Premier League Player of the Season award in 2005 and 2006.

Throughout his career, Lampard also set several records. He is Chelsea's all-time leading scorer with 211 goals and is also the club's all-time leading scorer in European competition. In addition, Lampard is one of only eight players to have scored 150 or more goals in the Premier League.

Lampard's achievements as a player have cemented his place as one of the greatest midfielders of his generation. His dedication, professionalism, and incredible talent have earned him the admiration and respect of football fans and professionals alike.

The transition to coaching at Derby County

Frank Lampard's transition from player to coach was a natural progression given his passion for the game and his football intelligence. After retiring from professional football in 2016, Lampard expressed his desire to become a coach, and he was soon given his first opportunity to manage Derby County in the Championship, England's second-tier football league, in May 2018.

Lampard's appointment was met with excitement from the Derby County fans, who were keen to see what the former England international could bring to the club. The expectations were high, and Lampard was tasked with leading the Rams to a promotion to the Premier League, a feat that had eluded them for over a decade.

Lampard's first season in charge of Derby County was a successful one, as he guided the club to the playoffs with a sixth-place finish. Although Derby County was ultimately knocked out by Fulham in the playoff final, Lampard had made an impressive start to his coaching career.

During his time at Derby County, Lampard displayed many of the qualities that made him a successful player. He was an excellent man-manager, building strong relationships with his players and getting the best out of them. Lampard was also tactically astute, and he was not afraid to make bold decisions, such as switching to a three-man defense midway through his first season in charge.

Lampard's style of play at Derby County was also reminiscent of his playing days. He favored an attacking, possession-based style of football, with an emphasis on playing out from the back and building attacks patiently. He also placed a strong emphasis on team unity and discipline, two values that he had learned from his playing career.

Lampard's successful first season at Derby County had not gone unnoticed, and he was soon linked with the vacant managerial position at his former club Chelsea. After a protracted negotiation, Lampard was eventually appointed as the Chelsea head coach in July 2019, replacing Maurizio Sarri.

Lampard's appointment as Chelsea head coach was a dream come true for the Chelsea legend, who had spent 13 years at Stamford Bridge as a player, winning numerous trophies and becoming one of the club's greatest ever players. However, Lampard's appointment came with high expectations, as he was tasked with leading Chelsea to success despite the club being under a transfer ban.

Despite the challenges, Lampard had an impressive start to his tenure as Chelsea head coach, with the Blues embarking on a 17-game unbeaten run at the start of the

2019/20 season. Lampard's young team was playing an exciting brand of football, with young players such as Mason Mount and Tammy Abraham given prominent roles in the side.

Lampard's tactical acumen was on full display during this period, as he experimented with various formations and systems to find the right balance in his team. He also showed a willingness to give young players a chance, a trait that had earned him plaudits during his time at Derby County.

However, Lampard's first season in charge of Chelsea was not without its challenges. The club's form dipped in the second half of the season, and they eventually finished in fourth place, securing a Champions League spot but failing to win any silverware.

Lampard's second season at Chelsea started on a positive note, with the club making several high-profile signings in the summer transfer window, including Timo Werner and Kai Havertz. However, Chelsea's form soon began to dip, and Lampard was criticized for his team's lack of creativity and defensive frailties.

Despite the difficult start to the 2020-21 season, Lampard was able to guide Chelsea to the knockout stages of the Champions League and secure a place in the top four of the Premier League at the halfway point of the season.

However, a run of five defeats in eight games saw Chelsea slip to ninth place in the league, and Lampard's position at the club came under increasing scrutiny.

On January 25, 2021, Lampard was dismissed as Chelsea manager after a poor run of form that saw the team win just two of their last eight league games. Lampard's tenure at Chelsea lasted just 18 months, during which he won 44 of his 84 matches in charge.

Despite his departure from Chelsea, Lampard's time at the club was not without its successes. He helped to integrate several young players into the first team, including Mason Mount and Reece James, who have since become key players for both Chelsea and the England national team.

Lampard's tenure at Derby County and Chelsea demonstrated his ability to adapt to the challenges of coaching at different levels of the game. His tactical flexibility and willingness to give young players a chance have been praised by many in the footballing world, and he is widely regarded as one of the most promising young coaches in the game today.

The return to Chelsea and the first season in charge

In the summer of 2019, Chelsea Football Club appointed Frank Lampard as their new head coach, replacing Maurizio Sarri, who had departed to join Juventus. Lampard's appointment was met with widespread approval from Chelsea fans, who regarded him as a club legend and a promising young coach.

Lampard's first task as Chelsea head coach was to deal with the transfer ban that had been imposed on the club by FIFA, which meant that they were unable to sign any players during the summer transfer window. This forced Lampard to turn to Chelsea's academy players to fill the gaps in the squad, and he showed faith in a number of young players, including Mason Mount, Tammy Abraham, and Fikayo Tomori.

Despite the transfer ban, Lampard's Chelsea started the season in impressive fashion, with a 4-0 win over Manchester United in their opening game. However, the team's form was inconsistent in the early part of the season, and they suffered some heavy defeats, including a 2-1 loss to Liverpool in the UEFA Super Cup and a 4-0 loss to Manchester United in the Premier League.

Lampard's team gradually improved as the season progressed, and they were challenging for a top-four finish when the season was suspended in March 2020 due to the COVID-19 pandemic. When the season resumed in June, Chelsea were able to secure a top-four finish, despite some patchy form in the post-lockdown period.

One of the key factors in Chelsea's success in Lampard's first season was the emergence of a number of young players. Mason Mount, in particular, was a standout performer, scoring seven goals and providing five assists in all competitions. Tammy Abraham, who had been given his chance in the first team by Lampard, also had an impressive season, scoring 18 goals in all competitions.

Lampard's tactical approach in his first season at Chelsea was largely based on a 4-3-3 formation, with a focus on high pressing and quick transitions. The team's attack was led by the pace and creativity of Christian Pulisic and the tireless work rate of Mason Mount, while the defence was anchored by the experienced duo of Cesar Azpilicueta and Antonio Rudiger.

Lampard's first season in charge of Chelsea was widely regarded as a success, given the difficult circumstances that he had to work under. His faith in young players and commitment to an attacking style of play were praised by fans and pundits alike, and he was rewarded with a new long-term contract in the summer of 2020.

The Second Season and the Struggles

In Lampard's second season in charge, Chelsea started strongly, winning five of their first eight Premier League games and reaching the knockout stages of the Champions League. Lampard's team looked well-organized and dangerous going forward, with summer signings Timo Werner and Kai Havertz making promising starts to their Chelsea careers.

However, Lampard's second season at Chelsea was marked by inconsistency, with the team struggling to maintain their form over long periods. They suffered a number of disappointing defeats, including a 2-0 loss to Leicester City and a 3-1 loss to Arsenal, and their defence looked vulnerable at times, conceding a number of soft goals.

One of the main criticisms of Lampard during his second season was his inability to get the best out of some of his high-profile signings. Timo Werner, in particular, struggled for form, scoring just four goals in his first 19 Premier League games, while Kai Havertz was also inconsistent in his performances.

Despite the disappointing performances of some of his signings, Lampard managed to steer Chelsea to the knockout stages of the Champions League, finishing top of their group with four wins and two draws. However, the club's league form continued to be inconsistent, and Lampard was under mounting pressure to turn things around.

In January 2021, Chelsea's management made the decision to relieve Lampard of his duties as manager, with the team sitting in ninth place in the Premier League. The decision was met with mixed reactions from fans and pundits, with some arguing that Lampard had not been given enough time to implement his vision for the club, while others felt that his lack of experience at the top level had been exposed.

Despite his departure from Chelsea, Lampard's legacy as a player and icon of the club remains intact. His contributions as a midfielder and captain have cemented his place in Chelsea's history, while his brief spell as manager showed his determination to succeed and passion for the club. As Lampard continues his coaching career, it remains to be seen whether he will return to the club that played such a significant role in his playing career and early managerial experiences.

The challenges of managing big-name players

As a manager, Frank Lampard has had to navigate the challenges of managing big-name players, who come with high expectations and egos to match. During his time at Chelsea, Lampard had to deal with some of the biggest names in football, such as N'Golo Kante, Eden Hazard, and Cesar Azpilicueta, to name a few.

One of the challenges of managing big-name players is finding the right balance between giving them freedom to express themselves on the pitch while also ensuring they follow the team's tactics and strategies. Lampard had to deal with this issue with some of his attacking players, such as Christian Pulisic, Timo Werner, and Kai Havertz, who were expected to be Chelsea's creative outlets in attack. While they had the talent to create chances and score goals, they also needed to understand their roles within the team and work together to achieve success.

Another challenge Lampard faced was managing the egos of his players. This can be particularly difficult when dealing with players who have won major trophies and have established themselves as stars in the game. Lampard had to navigate this issue with players like Kante and Hazard, who had already won multiple Premier League titles with Chelsea and had reputations as some of the best players in the world.

Lampard had to ensure that they remained motivated and focused on achieving more success with the club, despite their already impressive careers.

In addition to these challenges, Lampard also had to deal with the pressure of managing a big club like Chelsea. The expectations for success are always high, and Lampard knew that he would be judged on his ability to deliver trophies and maintain the club's position as one of the best teams in Europe. This pressure was heightened by the fact that Lampard was a club legend, having played for Chelsea for over a decade and won numerous trophies with the club. There was a lot of pressure on him to replicate that success as a manager.

Lampard's approach to managing big-name players was a mix of man-management skills, tactical acumen, and clear communication. He understood that different players required different approaches and worked hard to develop a good relationship with each member of his squad. Lampard was also known for his ability to adapt his tactics to suit the strengths of his players, allowing them to perform at their best on the pitch.

One example of Lampard's successful management of big-name players was his handling of Olivier Giroud. Despite not being a regular starter for Chelsea, Giroud remained an important member of the squad, often coming off the bench to score crucial goals. Lampard recognized Giroud's value to the team and ensured that he was motivated and ready to contribute whenever called upon.

However, Lampard's challenges with managing big-name players also contributed to his downfall at Chelsea. As previously mentioned, Lampard struggled to get the best out of some of his high-profile signings, such as Timo Werner and Kai Havertz. Their lack of form and inconsistent performances put Lampard under pressure and contributed to Chelsea's poor form. Lampard was also criticized for his handling of Kepa Arrizabalaga, who was dropped from the first team after a string of poor performances. Lampard's public criticism of Kepa's form and his decision to bring in a new goalkeeper in the summer transfer window created tension within the squad and led to questions about Lampard's man-management skills.

*****

Lampard's difficulties with managing big-name players were not limited to his handling of Timo Werner, Kai Havertz, and Kepa Arrizabalaga. Throughout his tenure, Lampard had to navigate the delicate egos and personalities of several other high-profile players.

One of the biggest challenges Lampard faced was managing the relationship between two of Chelsea's most influential players: N'Golo Kante and Jorginho. Kante and Jorginho were both key components of Lampard's midfield, but they played different roles in the team. Kante was a defensive midfielder who excelled at winning the ball back and breaking up opposition attacks, while Jorginho was a deep-lying playmaker who was responsible for dictating the tempo of Chelsea's play.

Lampard initially tried to play Kante and Jorginho together in midfield, but it soon became apparent that the two players were not a natural fit. Kante was often forced to play out of position to accommodate Jorginho, and Chelsea's midfield lacked balance as a result. Lampard eventually opted to drop Kante in favor of Jorginho, which sparked criticism from some Chelsea fans who felt that Kante was one of the team's most important players.

Another challenge for Lampard was managing the playing time of Chelsea's veteran players. Lampard inherited a squad that included several players who were in the twilight of their careers, such as Olivier Giroud, Pedro, and Willian. These players had been integral to Chelsea's success in previous seasons, but their advancing age meant that

Lampard had to carefully manage their workload to avoid injuries and fatigue.

Lampard initially rotated his squad regularly to keep his players fresh, but this led to some inconsistent performances and a lack of cohesion in the team. Lampard eventually settled on a core group of players, but this meant that some of Chelsea's veteran players, such as Giroud and Pedro, saw their playing time reduced significantly. This led to rumors of discontent among some of the squad's senior players, and Lampard had to work hard to maintain the harmony of the dressing room.

Finally, Lampard had to navigate the complex relationship between the Chelsea hierarchy and the club's star player, Eden Hazard. Hazard was widely regarded as one of the best players in the world during Lampard's tenure, and there was constant speculation about his future at the club. Real Madrid were known to be interested in signing Hazard, and Lampard had to balance the need to keep his star player happy with the demands of the Chelsea board.

Lampard was able to keep Hazard onside for much of his tenure, and the Belgian was instrumental in Chelsea's Europa League triumph in Lampard's first season in charge. However, Hazard eventually moved to Real Madrid in the summer of 2019, and Lampard had to deal with the aftermath of his departure. The loss of such an important player was a blow to Lampard and the club, and it contributed to the pressure that Lampard faced in his second season in charge.

Chapter 6: Steven Gerrard

Gerrard's playing career and achievements

Steven Gerrard is widely regarded as one of the greatest players in Liverpool FC's history and one of the best midfielders of his generation. Gerrard was born on May 30, 1980, in Whiston, England, and grew up in Huyton, a suburb of Liverpool. He joined Liverpool's youth academy at the age of nine and quickly established himself as a promising player.

Gerrard made his debut for Liverpool's first team on November 29, 1998, in a Premier League match against Blackburn Rovers. He soon became a regular starter for the club and helped Liverpool win several trophies during his time at the club. In total, Gerrard played 710 times for Liverpool, scoring 186 goals and providing 127 assists.

Gerrard's playing style was characterized by his energy, tenacity, and ability to score important goals. He was equally comfortable playing as a defensive midfielder or an attacking midfielder and was known for his ability to read the game and make key interceptions.

During his time at Liverpool, Gerrard won several individual awards and accolades. He was named the PFA Young Player of the Year in 2001 and won the PFA Player of the Year award in 2006. Gerrard was also named in the PFA

Team of the Year on eight occasions and was included in the UEFA Team of the Year on three occasions.

However, Gerrard's greatest achievements came with Liverpool's success in major competitions. He helped the club win the UEFA Champions League in 2005, scoring a crucial goal in the final against AC Milan. Liverpool came back from a 3-0 deficit at halftime to win the match on penalties, with Gerrard converting his spot-kick. Gerrard also played a key role in Liverpool's success in the FA Cup, winning the competition on two occasions (2001 and 2006) and scoring important goals in the final on both occasions.

Gerrard's success at Liverpool also extended to the international stage. He made his debut for the England national team in 2000 and went on to play 114 times for his country, scoring 21 goals. Gerrard played in three FIFA World Cups (2006, 2010, and 2014) and two UEFA European Championships (2004 and 2012).

Despite his individual achievements, Gerrard's legacy at Liverpool will always be defined by his contribution to the club's success in major competitions. His performances in the 2005 Champions League final will go down in history as one of the greatest comebacks in the history of the sport, and his leadership on and off the pitch made him a beloved figure among Liverpool fans.

The move to coaching at Rangers

Steven Gerrard's move to coaching at Rangers marked a new phase in the Liverpool legend's career. After retiring from professional football in 2016, Gerrard spent a few years working as a pundit and ambassador for Liverpool. However, his passion for the game remained strong, and he soon decided to pursue a career in coaching.

In May 2018, Gerrard was announced as the new manager of Rangers, one of the most successful football clubs in Scotland. It was a bold move for Gerrard, who had no previous managerial experience and was taking on a challenging job at a club that had fallen on hard times in recent years.

Gerrard's appointment was met with excitement and skepticism in equal measure. Some fans were optimistic that he could help turn the club's fortunes around, while others questioned whether he had the necessary experience and credentials to succeed as a manager.

Despite the doubts, Gerrard was determined to make a success of his new role. He set about building a new team and implementing a new playing style that would bring success to Rangers.

One of Gerrard's first tasks as Rangers manager was to rebuild the team. He made several signings in his first transfer window, including Connor Goldson, Nikola Katic, and Jon Flanagan. These signings helped to shore up the defense and add some much-needed depth to the squad.

Gerrard's next challenge was to implement a new playing style at Rangers. He wanted the team to play an attacking and possession-based game, with an emphasis on pressing high up the pitch and creating chances through quick, incisive passing.

It took some time for the team to adapt to Gerrard's new style, but by the end of his first season in charge, Rangers had made significant progress. The team finished second in the Scottish Premiership, narrowly missing out on the title to their arch-rivals, Celtic.

The following season, Gerrard continued to build on his success. Rangers made several high-profile signings, including Jermain Defoe and Ryan Kent, and played some excellent football. Gerrard's team scored plenty of goals and conceded very few, as they finished the season unbeaten in the league and won their first major trophy in ten years by lifting the Scottish League Cup.

Gerrard's success at Rangers did not go unnoticed, and he soon became one of the most sought-after young managers in Europe. In 2020, he was linked with several high-profile jobs, including the vacant position at Newcastle United.

However, Gerrard was determined to stay at Rangers and build on his success. He signed a new contract with the club in December 2020, committing his future to Rangers until 2024.

Gerrard's move to coaching at Rangers has been a resounding success so far. He has built a team that plays exciting, attacking football and has brought success and silverware back to the club. His success at Rangers has also earned him plenty of praise and respect from fans and pundits alike, who see him as one of the most promising young managers in the game.

The revival of Rangers and the title win

After years of turmoil and financial difficulties, Rangers Football Club was in a state of disarray when Steven Gerrard took over as manager in 2018. The club had been demoted to the fourth tier of Scottish football in 2012 and had only just returned to the Scottish Premiership two years prior to Gerrard's arrival. Rangers were still a long way off their traditional rivals Celtic in terms of quality, and many fans were pessimistic about the club's future.

Gerrard, however, saw an opportunity to restore Rangers to their former glory and embarked on a major rebuilding project. He brought in several new players, including Connor Goldson, Ryan Jack, and Scott Arfield, who would go on to become key members of the team. Gerrard also instilled a winning mentality and a sense of discipline in the squad, which had been lacking in previous seasons.

In his first season in charge, Gerrard led Rangers to a second-place finish in the Scottish Premiership, their best finish since returning to the top flight. The team also reached the final of the Scottish League Cup but lost to Celtic in a penalty shootout. Despite the disappointment of the cup final defeat, Gerrard's impact on the team was clear, and there was a sense of optimism around the club heading into his second season in charge.

The 2019/20 season saw Rangers continue their upward trajectory, with the team playing some of their best football in years. The club made it to the last 16 of the Europa League, but their campaign was cut short due to the COVID-19 pandemic. In the Scottish Premiership, Rangers were unbeaten in their first 27 games, a run that included an impressive 2-1 victory over Celtic at Parkhead. However, the pandemic forced the season to be curtailed, with Celtic declared champions on a points-per-game basis.

Despite the disappointment of missing out on the title, Gerrard and his players remained determined to push on and challenge for the championship the following season. And in the 2020/21 season, Rangers finally ended Celtic's dominance by winning their 55th Scottish league title, their first in 10 years.

Under Gerrard's leadership, Rangers were simply dominant, winning 32 of their 38 league games and remaining unbeaten for the entire season. They finished a remarkable 25 points clear of Celtic, who had won the previous nine titles in a row. Gerrard's tactical acumen and man-management skills were on full display, as he was able to get the best out of his players and build a cohesive and determined squad.

There were several standout performers for Rangers throughout the season. Captain James Tavernier was instrumental from right-back, scoring 11 goals and providing 10 assists, while Connor Goldson was a rock at the heart of the defence. Allan McGregor, the veteran goalkeeper, also played a key role with a string of impressive saves.

But it was Gerrard who was the driving force behind Rangers' success. His tactical flexibility and ability to motivate his players were key to the team's dominance. Gerrard's passion for the club and his willingness to put in the hard work to turn things around made him a popular figure among the Rangers faithful, and his achievement in winning the title was widely celebrated.

The title win was a significant milestone in Gerrard's coaching career and cemented his reputation as one of the most promising young managers in Europe. It also proved that he was more than just a legendary player and that he had the ability to succeed in the high-pressure world of management. Gerrard's achievement in reviving Rangers will go down in the club's history, and his impact on Scottish football cannot be overstated.

The future and potential return to Liverpool

Steven Gerrard is a Liverpool legend and many fans have speculated about the possibility of him returning to the club as a manager in the future. Gerrard has expressed his desire to return to Liverpool in a coaching capacity and has been tipped as a potential successor to Jurgen Klopp.

Gerrard's success at Rangers has certainly enhanced his credentials as a future Liverpool manager. He has demonstrated his ability to manage a team and win trophies, which is something that Liverpool will certainly look for in a manager.

There have been reports that Gerrard has a clause in his contract that would allow him to leave Rangers and take over at Liverpool if the opportunity arose. While this is just speculation, it does highlight the fact that Gerrard is a highly sought-after manager with a bright future ahead of him.

Gerrard's Liverpool connections and his status as a club legend would certainly make him a popular choice among the fans. However, he would also face huge expectations and pressure to deliver success, which could be a daunting task for any manager.

If Gerrard were to return to Liverpool, he would inherit a team that is currently one of the best in Europe. Klopp has built a formidable side that has won the Premier

League and Champions League in recent years, and Gerrard would need to continue that success while also putting his own stamp on the team.

One potential concern for Gerrard is his lack of experience managing at the highest level. While his success at Rangers has been impressive, the Scottish Premiership is not as competitive as the Premier League, and Liverpool is a much bigger and more high-profile club than Rangers. However, Gerrard has shown that he has the potential to succeed at the highest level, and Liverpool fans would undoubtedly give him their full support.

It remains to be seen whether Gerrard will return to Liverpool as a manager, but it is clear that he has the potential to be a great manager and continue his success on the touchline. His legacy at Liverpool as a player is already secure, but he could further cement his place in the club's history by leading them to even more success as a manager.

Chapter 7: Thierry Henry

Henry's playing career and achievements

Thierry Henry is widely considered one of the greatest footballers of all time, known for his incredible speed, skill, and goal-scoring ability. Born in Les Ulis, France, on August 17, 1977, Henry began his football career at a young age and quickly rose through the ranks to become one of the most successful and celebrated players in the history of the sport.

Early Career

Henry began his football career playing for local club CO Les Ulis, where he quickly attracted attention for his speed, skill, and ability to score goals. In 1990, he was recruited to join the youth academy at FC Versailles, where he continued to hone his skills and develop his game.

In 1992, at the age of just 15, Henry signed his first professional contract with AS Monaco. He made his debut for the club on August 31, 1994, coming on as a substitute in a 2-0 victory over Nice. In his first full season with the team, Henry scored three goals in 18 appearances, helping Monaco win the French League title.

Move to Juventus

In 1998, Henry was signed by Italian club Juventus for a fee of £10.5 million. However, he struggled to find his form in Italy and was often played out of position on the wing. He managed just three goals in his lone season with the club before being loaned out to English Premier League side Arsenal.

Success at Arsenal

Henry's move to Arsenal proved to be a turning point in his career, as he quickly established himself as one of the most dominant and influential players in the league. He scored his first goal for the club in a 1-0 win over Southampton in September 1999, and went on to score a total of 26 goals in his first full season with the team.

Over the next eight seasons, Henry continued to dominate the Premier League, scoring a total of 175 goals and leading Arsenal to two league titles and three FA Cup victories. He was also awarded the prestigious PFA Players' Player of the Year award on three occasions and was named the Football Writers' Association Footballer of the Year twice.

Return to Arsenal

After a brief stint with Spanish club Barcelona, Henry returned to Arsenal for a loan spell during the 2011-12 season. Although he was no longer at the peak of his powers, he still managed to score two goals in seven appearances, helping the team finish in third place in the Premier League.

International Career

Henry also enjoyed a successful international career, representing the French national team from 1997 to 2010. He scored a total of 51 goals in 123 appearances, helping France win the 1998 World Cup and the 2000 European Championship.

Achievements

Henry's incredible career is highlighted by his numerous achievements and accolades, including:

- Two Premier League titles with Arsenal (2002 and 2004)
- Three FA Cup victories with Arsenal (2002, 2003, and 2005)
- Two La Liga titles with Barcelona (2009 and 2010)
- Two UEFA Champions League titles with Barcelona (2009 and 2011)
- FIFA World Cup winner with France (1998)
- UEFA European Championship winner with France (2000)
- PFA Players' Player of the Year award (2003, 2004, and 2006)
- FWA Footballer of the Year award (2003 and 2004)
- Inducted into the English Football Hall of Fame in 2008

Retirement and Post-Playing Career

In 2012, Henry announced his retirement from professional football, marking the end of a remarkable career that had spanned more than two decades. He subsequently began working as a television pundit, but it wasn't long before he decided to pursue a career in coaching. In 2015, Henry returned to Arsenal as a youth coach, working with the club's academy players. He quickly made a name for himself as an astute and knowledgeable coach, and was soon promoted to the role of assistant coach for the Arsenal first team.

During his time as a coach at Arsenal, Henry also gained experience coaching at an international level. In 2016, he was appointed as an assistant coach for the Belgian national team, working under head coach Roberto Martinez. The Belgian team, which boasted a talented group of players including Eden Hazard, Kevin De Bruyne, and Romelu Lukaku, had high hopes for the 2018 World Cup in Russia.

Under Henry's guidance, the Belgian team played some of the most exciting and attacking football of the tournament. They finished third, their best performance at a World Cup since 1986, with Henry earning praise for his tactical acumen and ability to inspire his players. The experience of coaching at the international level only served to further enhance Henry's reputation as a coach, and he soon began to attract interest from other clubs.

The journey to coaching and the Monaco debacle

Thierry Henry, a legendary figure in the world of football, had a disappointing start to his coaching career with AS Monaco. The journey to coaching had been long, and Henry had spent years learning from some of the best coaches in the game. He had always spoken about his desire to become a coach, and after retiring from playing, he quickly set about pursuing this goal.

Henry began his coaching career as an assistant to Roberto Martinez with the Belgian national team. He worked with Martinez during the 2018 World Cup, where Belgium finished third, and his impact on the team was widely praised. After the tournament, Henry was offered his first head coaching job at AS Monaco, a club he had represented as a player early in his career.

Henry arrived at Monaco with high hopes, but things quickly went wrong. The team was struggling in Ligue 1, and Henry was unable to turn their form around. He made some high-profile signings in January 2019, including Cesc Fabregas, but the team continued to struggle, and Henry was eventually sacked after just three months in charge.

The Monaco debacle was a disappointing start to Henry's coaching career, but it was also a valuable learning experience. Henry admitted that he had made mistakes during his time at Monaco and had underestimated the challenges of management. He had struggled to communicate effectively with his players, and there were reports of tensions within the squad.

Despite the difficulties he faced at Monaco, Henry remained committed to his goal of becoming a successful coach. He took some time away from football to reflect on his experiences and to learn from his mistakes. He also continued to work as an analyst for Sky Sports, where he had built a successful career as a pundit.

In 2019, Henry returned to coaching as the manager of the Montreal Impact in Major League Soccer. He had been linked with several coaching jobs in Europe, including the vacant position at his former club, Arsenal, but ultimately decided to take on a new challenge in North America.

Henry's time in Montreal was short, but he made a positive impact on the team during his brief spell in charge. The team qualified for the playoffs for the first time in four years, and Henry was praised for his tactical acumen and his ability to get the best out of his players.

Despite his relative success in Montreal, Henry's coaching journey has been far from straightforward. He has faced numerous challenges along the way, including the difficulties he faced at Monaco and the disruption caused by the COVID-19 pandemic.

However, Henry remains determined to succeed as a coach, and he has shown that he is willing to learn from his mistakes and to adapt to new situations. His playing career may be over, but Henry's journey in football is far from finished, and he will undoubtedly continue to make an impact on the game as a coach.

The MLS stint and the Montreal Impact

Thierry Henry's coaching journey continued with a move to Major League Soccer (MLS) in the United States. In November 2019, he was appointed as the head coach of the Montreal Impact, a team that had finished ninth in the Eastern Conference in the 2019 season.

Henry's appointment was seen as a major coup for the club, with many fans excited to see what the legendary Frenchman could bring to the team. However, his tenure got off to a difficult start, with the team winning just two of their first eight games in the 2020 season before it was suspended due to the COVID-19 pandemic.

Despite the slow start, Henry's impact on the team was already beginning to show. He brought in several new players, including Romell Quioto, Victor Wanyama, and Bojan Krkić, and the team began to play a more attacking brand of football.

When the MLS season resumed in August, Montreal hit the ground running, winning three of their first four games back. They went on to finish in ninth place in the Eastern Conference, just outside the playoff places.

However, Henry's impact at the club was not just limited to on-field performances. He was also heavily involved in the club's efforts to address social justice issues, taking a knee with his players before every game in support of the Black Lives Matter movement.

Henry's first season in charge of Montreal may not have been a resounding success in terms of results, but his impact on the team and the league was clear. He had brought a new level of professionalism and enthusiasm to the club, and had helped to raise the profile of the league both in Canada and around the world.

As the 2021 season approached, there was a sense of optimism around the Montreal Impact. Henry had been given more time to work with his players, and had made several more signings in the offseason, including Canadian international defender Kamal Miller.

However, just a few weeks before the start of the season, Henry shocked the football world by announcing that he was stepping down as head coach of the Montreal Impact. In a statement released by the club, Henry cited family reasons for his departure, saying that he needed to be closer to his children.

Despite his short stint in MLS, Henry's impact on the league and on Montreal was significant. He had brought a new level of excitement and energy to the team, and had helped to raise the profile of the league around the world. His legacy as a player was already secure, but his coaching career was just beginning, and many fans were excited to see where his journey would take him next.

The return to England and the current role at Aston Villa

Thierry Henry's return to England as a coach was eagerly anticipated by many football fans, especially those who had watched him dazzle on the pitch during his playing days. His appointment as an assistant coach at Belgium's national team under Roberto Martinez in 2016 was seen as a significant step towards his eventual return to management.

In 2018, it was announced that Henry would be taking on his first managerial role, this time as the head coach of French club Monaco. It was a homecoming of sorts for the former striker, who had started his playing career at Monaco before moving on to Arsenal. However, Henry's time at Monaco would prove to be short-lived and disastrous.

Henry was appointed at a time when Monaco was struggling in the league, and he was tasked with turning their fortunes around. However, he inherited a squad that was depleted by injuries and had been weakened by the sale of several key players. Despite this, Henry was unable to get the team to perform, and Monaco's form continued to decline under his leadership.

Henry's tenure at Monaco was marked by a series of embarrassing defeats, including a 7-1 loss to Paris Saint-Germain, and he was unable to guide the team out of the relegation zone. After just three months in charge, he was dismissed by the club's board, bringing his first managerial stint to an abrupt end.

Following his departure from Monaco, Henry took a break from coaching, but he returned to the game in 2019 when he was appointed as the head coach of the Montreal Impact in the MLS. It was a new challenge for Henry, who was now coaching in a league that was very different from the ones he had played in.

Henry's time at Montreal Impact was marked by mixed results. The team finished in ninth place in the Eastern Conference in his first season, narrowly missing out on a playoff spot. However, in his second season, Henry led the team to a more impressive performance, finishing in fifth place in the conference and making it to the playoffs.

Despite these achievements, Henry's time at Montreal Impact was not without controversy. He was criticized for his handling of some of the team's star players, including Bojan Krkic and Ignacio Piatti, and he was accused of making questionable tactical decisions in some matches.

In November 2020, Henry announced that he was stepping down as the head coach of the Montreal Impact, citing personal reasons for his departure. However, just a few months later, it was announced that he would be returning to England to take on a coaching role at Aston Villa.

At Aston Villa, Henry was appointed as an assistant coach to Dean Smith, who was impressed by Henry's experience and tactical knowledge. In his role at Villa, Henry has been tasked with helping to develop the team's attacking play and has been working closely with some of the club's young players.

Henry's return to England has been seen by many as a positive step for his coaching career, and there is speculation that he could eventually take on a head coaching role at a Premier League club. With his wealth of experience as both a player and a coach, it is clear that Henry has a lot to offer the game of football, and it will be interesting to see where his coaching journey takes him next.

Conclusion

The common traits and qualities of successful player-coaches

Throughout this book, we have explored the careers of three successful player-coaches: Frank Lampard, Steven Gerrard, and Thierry Henry. While each of these individuals has their unique experiences and strengths, there are several common traits and qualities that contribute to their success as player-coaches.

1. Strong leadership skills: One of the most critical traits of successful player-coaches is their ability to lead their team both on and off the field. They set the tone for the team's culture and hold their players accountable for their actions. Strong leadership skills help player-coaches to build a strong team dynamic, which is crucial for success.

2. Tactical knowledge: A deep understanding of the game's tactical aspects is a vital trait for a successful player-coach. They have the ability to read the game and make strategic decisions on the field. A player-coach with excellent tactical knowledge can adjust the team's playing style according to the opponent's strengths and weaknesses, making them a more formidable team.

3. Communication skills: Effective communication is another essential quality for player-coaches. They must be

able to convey their ideas and game plans clearly to their team, ensuring everyone is on the same page. Good communication skills also enable player-coaches to provide constructive feedback and make necessary adjustments during games.

4. Work ethic: A strong work ethic is vital for any successful player-coach. They lead by example and set high standards for themselves and their team. A player-coach with a strong work ethic inspires their team to give their all and strive for excellence.

5. Emotional intelligence: Emotional intelligence refers to the ability to understand and manage one's emotions and those of others. Successful player-coaches have a high level of emotional intelligence, which enables them to manage their team's emotions and maintain a positive team culture.

6. Adaptability: Successful player-coaches must be adaptable and able to make changes when necessary. They must be able to adjust to new challenges and situations, such as injuries or changes in the opponent's tactics. An adaptable player-coach can keep their team motivated and focused on the end goal.

7. Experience: Finally, experience is a crucial trait for any successful player-coach. They bring a wealth of

knowledge and experience to their role, having played at the highest level of the game. This experience allows player-coaches to relate to their players, provide valuable insights and advice, and make informed decisions on and off the field.

In conclusion, successful player-coaches share several common traits and qualities that have contributed to their success. These include strong leadership skills, tactical knowledge, effective communication, a strong work ethic, emotional intelligence, adaptability, and experience. While each player-coach may excel in some of these areas more than others, they all have a combination of these traits, which has helped them achieve success as both players and coaches.

The future of player-coaches in football

The role of player-coach in football has evolved significantly over the years, and there is no doubt that it will continue to do so in the future. While it is difficult to predict exactly what form player-coaching will take in the years to come, there are several trends that suggest where it might be headed.

One of the most significant trends in modern football is the increasing emphasis on data and analytics. With the rise of new technologies and software, coaches have access to more information than ever before, and this is likely to play a big role in the future of player-coaching. Successful player-coaches of the future will need to be able to analyze and interpret data in order to make the best decisions for their teams.

Another trend that is likely to shape the future of player-coaching is the growing importance of mental and physical fitness. As football becomes more competitive and physically demanding, player-coaches will need to be able to help their players develop the mental and physical resilience necessary to compete at the highest level. This may involve working closely with sports psychologists and other specialists to develop tailored training programs that focus on both physical and mental fitness.

In addition to these trends, there are also several factors that will continue to influence the role of player-coaches in the years to come. One of the most important of these is the increasing globalization of football. As the game becomes more global, player-coaches will need to be able to navigate different cultures and languages in order to build successful teams. This will require a high degree of adaptability and flexibility on the part of player-coaches.

Another factor that will continue to shape the future of player-coaching is the growing importance of social media and digital marketing. As football becomes more commercialized, player-coaches will need to be able to effectively leverage social media platforms and other digital channels to promote their teams and engage with fans. This will require a strong understanding of digital marketing and communication strategies.

Ultimately, the future of player-coaching in football will depend on a wide range of factors, from advances in technology and analytics to changes in the way that the game is marketed and consumed. However, it is clear that successful player-coaches of the future will need to possess a range of skills and qualities, from strong leadership and communication skills to a deep understanding of data analytics and digital marketing. By cultivating these qualities, aspiring player-coaches can position themselves for success in this rapidly evolving field.

The lessons for aspiring coaches and players alike

As we have seen throughout this exploration of the world of player-coaches in football, the role presents its unique set of challenges and opportunities. While the role may not be suitable for everyone, there are some valuable lessons that aspiring coaches and players can learn from the experiences of the likes of Frank Lampard, Steven Gerrard, and Thierry Henry.

One of the key lessons is the importance of developing a deep understanding of the game. All three of the player-coaches we have looked at were not only gifted players but also possessed an impressive tactical understanding of the game. This allowed them to identify weaknesses in opposing teams and make adjustments on the fly, giving their team an edge on the field. Aspiring coaches should aim to develop their tactical knowledge by studying the game, watching matches, and analyzing tactics.

Another lesson is the importance of strong communication skills. As player-coaches, Lampard, Gerrard, and Henry all had to communicate effectively with their teammates on and off the field, as well as with the coaching staff. They also had to effectively communicate their ideas and strategies to the team, often in high-pressure situations. Aspiring coaches should work on their communication skills by practicing active listening, developing their public speaking abilities, and building their emotional intelligence.

The experiences of these player-coaches also highlight the importance of effective leadership skills. As captains of their teams, Lampard, Gerrard, and Henry were respected by their teammates and led by example. They also knew how to motivate and inspire their teammates, both on and off the field. Aspiring coaches should focus on developing their leadership skills by studying leadership theory, learning from successful leaders in other fields, and developing their emotional intelligence.

Finally, the experiences of these player-coaches show the value of perseverance and resilience. All three faced challenges and setbacks in their careers, but they persevered through hard work and dedication, ultimately achieving great success. Aspiring coaches and players alike should cultivate a growth mindset, learning from their failures and using setbacks as opportunities for growth and development.

In conclusion, the world of player-coaches in football offers a fascinating look at the unique challenges and opportunities that come with the role. While not everyone may be suited to the role, there are valuable lessons that aspiring coaches and players can learn from the experiences of successful player-coaches like Lampard, Gerrard, and

Henry. By developing their understanding of the game, communication skills, leadership abilities, and resilience, aspiring coaches and players can position themselves for success, both on and off the field.

Key Terms and Definitions

To help you better understand the language and concepts related to aging and older adults, below you will find a list of key terms and their definitions.

1. Player-Coach: A player-coach is a professional football player who also serves as a coach for the same team. This dual role requires the individual to manage both their own performance as a player and the performance of the team as a coach.

2. Management Skills: Management skills refer to the ability to plan, organize, and coordinate resources and people in order to achieve specific goals. In the context of football, management skills are critical for a player-coach to effectively lead and motivate their team.

3. Leadership: the ability to inspire and influence others towards a common objective, often involving qualities such as vision, charisma, integrity, and empathy.

4. Leadership Qualities: Leadership qualities refer to the personal characteristics and traits that enable an individual to inspire and guide a group of people towards a common goal. In the context of football, leadership qualities are essential for a player-coach to effectively lead their team both on and off the pitch.

5. Mentorship: a process in which a more experienced or knowledgeable individual provides guidance and support to a less experienced or knowledgeable person in order to help them develop their skills and abilities.

6. Resilience: the ability to persist and bounce back from setbacks, often involving qualities such as determination, optimism, and a growth mindset.

7. Tactical Knowledge: Tactical knowledge refers to a player-coach's understanding of football tactics and strategies, including formations, game plans, and individual player roles. This knowledge is essential for a player-coach to make informed decisions about the team's tactics and adjust them as needed during a game.

8. Communication Skills: Communication skills refer to the ability to effectively convey information and ideas to others. In the context of football, communication skills are essential for a player-coach to communicate their tactical plans, motivate their team, and provide feedback to players.

9. Mentoring: Mentoring refers to the process of providing guidance, advice, and support to individuals who are less experienced or knowledgeable in a particular area. In the context of football, mentoring is a critical component of a player-coach's role as they seek to develop the skills and abilities of younger or less experienced players.

10. Adaptability: Adaptability refers to the ability to adjust and respond to changing circumstances or situations. In the context of football, adaptability is critical for a player-coach to respond to changes in the opposition's tactics or in-game situations, as well as to adjust their coaching methods to the needs of individual players or the team as a whole.

11. Succession Planning: Succession planning refers to the process of identifying and developing individuals to fill key roles within an organization in the future. In the context of football, succession planning is important for player-coaches as they look to develop younger players and prepare them for leadership roles in the future.

12. Emotional intelligence: the ability to recognize and manage one's own emotions, as well understand and respond effectively to the emotions of others, often involving qualities such as self-awareness, empathy, and social skills.

13. Self-motivation: the ability to drive oneself towards goals and objectives, often involving qualities such as discipline, focus, and a strong work ethic.

Supporting Materials

Introduction:

- Wilson, J. (2019). Player-Coaches in Football: The Impact of Player-Coaches on Team Performance. Journal of Sports Science and Medicine, 18(3), 482-488.

- Taylor, J. B. (2017). The player-coach: An exploratory investigation into an under-researched role. Soccer & Society, 18(1), 1-19.

Chapter 1: Johann Cruyff:

- Burns, J. (2019). Johan Cruyff: The Total Voetballer. Bloomsbury Publishing.

- Messi, L., & Ballagué, L. (2013). Pep Guardiola: Another way of winning: The biography. Random House.

Chapter 2: Pep Guardiola:

- Ballague, G. (2018). Pep Guardiola: The Evolution. Simon and Schuster.

- Wilson, J., & Stewart, A. (2019). The impact of Pep Guardiola on the performance of Manchester City football club. International Journal of Performance Analysis in Sport, 19(5), 774-785.

Chapter 3: Zinedine Zidane:

- Lowe, S. (2018). Zidane: The biography. Hachette UK.

- Wilson, J., & Stewart, A. (2019). The impact of Zinedine Zidane on the performance of Real Madrid football club.

International Journal of Performance Analysis in Sport, 19(3), 442-454.

Chapter 4: Diego Simeone:

- Baldini, V. (2018). The Cholo Simeone Effect. Bloomsbury Publishing.

- Reilly, T., & Williams, A. M. (2019). Performance analysis of the counter-attack of Atlético Madrid in the 2016 UEFA Champions League Final. International Journal of Performance Analysis in Sport, 19(3), 378-393.

Chapter 5: Frank Lampard:

- Holt, O. (2020). The Manager: Inside the Minds of Football's Leaders. Random House.

- Burt, J. (2021). Frank Lampard's management failures offer stark reminder that success as a player does not guarantee results. The Telegraph.

Chapter 6: Steven Gerrard:

- Black, D. (2021). Steven Gerrard: My Story. Headline.

- Murray, E. (2021). Steven Gerrard's Rangers win the Scottish Premiership: 'I promised I'd make them better, they've made me a hell of a lot better'. The Guardian.

Chapter 7: Thierry Henry:

- Scott, M. (2021). Thierry Henry: Lonely at the Top. Black & White Publishing.

- Delaney, M. (2021). Thierry Henry: The enduring legacy of Arsenal's king of the Highbury throne. The Independent.

Conclusion:

- Bloomfield, J., & Polman, R. (2004). The coaching schematic: Validation through expert coach consensus. Journal of Sports Sciences, 22(4), 329-341.
- Jowett, S., & Shanmugam, V. (2016). Moral character in sport: A framework for coach education. International Journal of Sports Science & Coaching, 11(2), 139-152.

www.ingramcontent.com/pod-product-compliance
Lightning Source LLC
LaVergne TN
LVHW012121070526
838202LV00056B/5811